The Mermaid's Purse

TED HUGHES

The Mermaid's Purse

illustrated by Flora McDonnell

ALFRED A. KNOPF · NEW YORK

With grateful acknowledgment to R. J. Lloyd,
who suggested the title of the collection and whose
paintings were the inspiration behind many of the poems

THIS IS A BORZOI BOOK PUBLISHED BY ALFRED A. KNOPF, INC.

Text copyright © 1999 by The Estate of Ted Hughes
Illustrations copyright © 1999 by Flora McDonnell

KNOPF, BORZOI BOOKS, and the colophon are registered
trademarks of Random House, Inc.

www.randomhouse.com/kids

Library of Congress Cataloging-in-Publication Data
Hughes, Ted, 1930–1998.
The mermaid's purse / Ted Hughes ; illustrated by Flora McDonnell.
p.   cm.
Summary: A collection of poems about the creatures of the sea,
including the limpet, crab, and conger eel.
1. Marine animals—Juvenile poetry. 2. Children's poetry, English. 3. Sea poetry,
English. [1. Marine animals—Poetry. 2. English poetry.] I. McDonnell, Flora, ill.
II. Title.

PR6058.U37 M47 2000
821'.914—dc21
99-046098

ISBN 0-375-80569-9 (trade)
ISBN 0-375-90569-3 (lib. bdg.)

Printed in the United States of America
March 2000
10 9 8 7 6 5 4 3 2 1

CONTENTS

The Mermaid's Purse

Seal

Where Ocean heaved
A breast of silk
And a black jag reef
Boiled into milk

There bobbed up a head
With eyes as wild
And wide and dark
As a famine child.

I thought, by the way
It stared at me,
It had lost its mother
In the sea.

Gulls

Gulls are glanced from the lift
Of cliffing air
And left
Loitering in the descending drift,
Or tilt gradient and go
Down steep invisible clefts in the grain
Of air, blading against the blow,

Back-flip, wisp
Over the foam-galled green
Building seas, and they scissor
Tossed spray, shave sheen,
Wing-waltzing their shadows
Over the green hollows,

Or rise again in the wind's landward rush
And, hurdling the thundering bush
With the stone wall flung in their faces,
Repeat their graces.

Limpet

When big surf slams
His tower so hard
The Lighthouse-keeper's
Teeth are jarred

The Limpet laughs
Beneath her hat:
"There's nothing I love
So much as that!

"Huge seas of shock
That roar to knock me
Off my rocker
Rock me, rock me."

13

Mussel

When you prize
Her shells apart
To say Hello
The Mussel cries:
"I know! I know!
I confess
I am a mess.
But I'm all heart—
Heart that could not
Softer soften!

"An ugly girl,
But often, often
With a pearl."

Sea Anemone

For such a tender face
A touch is like a danger.
But the dance of my many arms
To the music of the sea
Brings many a friend to me.

None can resist my grace.
All fall for my charms.

Many a friend, many a stranger,
Many an enemy
Melts in my embrace.
I am anemone.

Blenny

Ocean's huge hammer
Shatters itself
All to forge
This wiry wee elf.

Cormorant

Drowned fishermen come back
As famished cormorants
With bare and freezing webby toes
Instead of boots and pants.

You've a hook at the end of your nose
You shiver all the day
Trying to dry your oilskin pajamas
Under the icy spray.

But worst—O worst of all—
The moment that you wish
For fried fish fingers in a flash
You're gagged with a frozen fish.

Pebbles

Where blown spray falls
We are the stones.

Of lands that burst
From sleep and bowed
Like animals
To slake their thirst
Where waters flowed
We are the bones.

Hermit Crab

The sea-bed's great—
But it's a plate.
Every fish
Watches this dish.

Just to be tough
Is not enough.
Some of the smart
Don't even start.

I stay in bed
With my house on my head,
Said the Hermit Crab,
Or go by cab.

Wreck

The sailors prayed to come to land
And their good ship's wreck soon made it,
And sat on the rocks like a one-man band
While the stormy sea still played it.

Now through many a winter's weathers
Many a summer hour
Under the cliff there blooms and withers
The sea's rare rust-flower.

Jellyfish

When my chandelier
Waltzes pulsing near
Let the swimmer fear.

Beached and bare
I'm less of a scare
But I don't care.

Though I look like a slob
It's a delicate job
Being just a blob.

Crab

In the low tide pools
I pack myself like
A handy pocket
Chest of tools.

But as the tide fills
Dancing I go
Under lifted veils
Tiptoe, tiptoe.

And with pliers and pincers
Repair and remake
The daintier dancers
The breakers break.

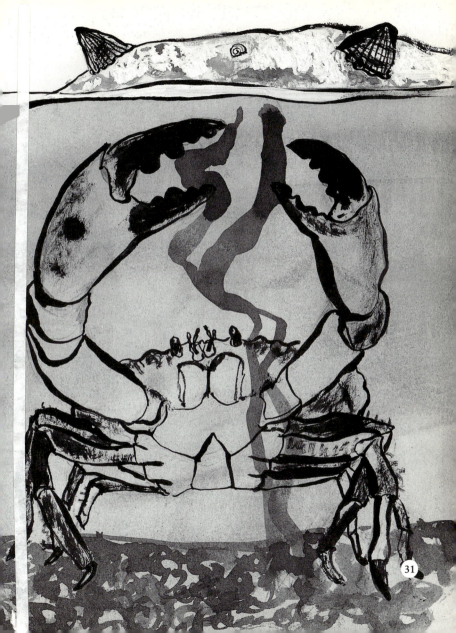

31

Mermaid

Call her a fish,
Call her a girl.
Call her the pearl

Of an oyster fresh
On its pearly dish

That the whole sea sips
With gurgly slurps
And sloppy lips.

Rag Worm

Rag Worm once
Was all the rage.
But suddenly, see
This foolish age
Of fish is in.
Fashion of flounce,
Of scale and slime,
Of scoot and squirm
And gill and fin
Gorping like fools.

Let future time
Be soon unfurled.

Bring all such schools
To end of term.

Return the world
To me, the Worm.

Sea Monster

Calm, empty sea
So soothes your eye
"Such peace!" you sigh—

Suddenly ME!

So huge, so near,
So really here,
Your stare goes dry
To see me come

So like a swan,
So slow, so high
You cannot cry

Already gone
Completely numb.

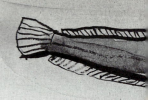

Whelk

I wonder whether
Whelks can wish?
If I were a Whelk
I think I'd sulk
To be a fish.

Though anything other
Than a screw
Of rubbery chew,
A gurgle of goo
Going down a drain
Would be a gain.

43

Shell

The sea fills my ear
With sand and with fear.

You may wash out the sand
But never the sound
Of the ghost of the sea
That is haunting me.

Octopus

"I am your bride,"
  The Octopus cried.
"O jump from your vessel!
  O dive with your muscle
  Through Ocean's rough bustle!
  Though I look like a tassel
  Of hideous gristle,
  A tussle of hassle,
  I'm a bundle of charms.
  O come, let us wrestle
  With noses a-jostle!
  You'll swoon in my arms
  With a sigh like a whistle—"

And she waved her arms, waiting,
Her colors pulsating
Like strobe lights rotating,

Her huge eyes dilating...

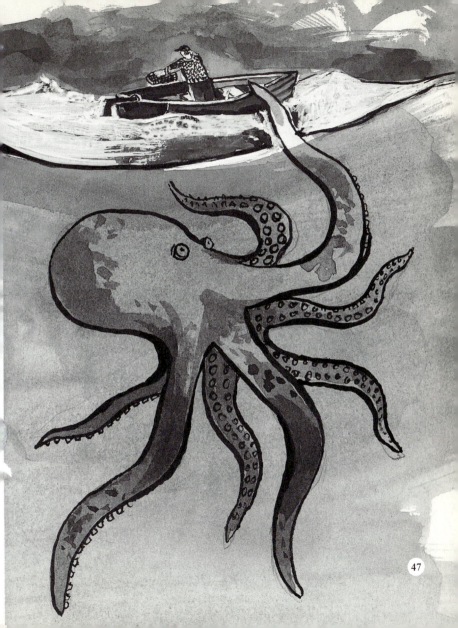

Heron

I am nothing
But a prayer
To catch a fish.
A hush of air—

A bloom of cloud
On a tilting stalk.
Over the water's face
I walk.

The little fishes
Tucked in under
Missing my flash
Sleep through my thunder.

Shrimp

The Shrimp sings: "The sea's
Ugliest weather
Merely preens
My glassy feather.

"I have the surf
As a rocking chair,
Combers to comb
My dainty hair,

"Though it's true my meat
Is a bit too sweet
And all who happen to meet me
Eat me."

Conger Eel

I am Conger
Out in the rough.
Long enough
But growing longer—
Thicker too.
A bit of a shock
At my cave-door
Beneath my rock.
But look at you—
You're not so thin.
As for my grin—
Your teeth are quite a
Good bit whiter
And eat more.

Flounder

The Flounder sees
Through crooked eyes.
Through crooked lips
The Flounder cries:

"While other fish flee
In goggling fright
From horrors below
And to left and to right

"I lie here
With a lovely feeling
Flat on my back
And gaze at the ceiling."

Bladder Wrack

The plastic rug
Of Bladder Wrack
Upsets the sea
With its oily black.

No matter how
The breakers drub it,
And boil their lather
And wring it and scrub it

Its rubbery pods
Dry out on the shore
Tougher and grubbier
Than before.

Whale

O hear the Whale's
Colossal song!
Suppler than any
Soprano's tongue

And wild as a hand
Among harp strings
Plunging through all
The seas she sings.

59

Sand Flea

"O see my eyes!"
  The Sand Flea cries,
"So beautiful,
  So blue, they make
  The sea seem dull."

But then she hides
Beneath the wrack.
She hears the tide's
Wild cry: "Give back
That China blue
I lent to you,"
As it sweeps blind hands
Of scrabbling suds
Across the sands.

Starfish

A Starfish stares
At stars that pour
Through depths of space
Without a shore.

She crimps her fingertips
And cries:
"If I could weep enough
Maybe
To rinse the salt
Out of my eyes
One of those dazzlers
Would be me!"

Ted Hughes, late poet laureate of Britain, was born in Mytholmroyd, Yorkshire, in 1930 and attended Cambridge University. A world-renowned poet, novelist, and essayist, he was also the author of many stories and poems for children, including the classic *The Iron Giant.* His last work, *Birthday Letters,* a volume of poetry chronicling his relationship with the American poet Sylvia Plath, was published shortly before his death in 1998 at the age of 68.